Foreword:

Prayers of Deliverance for Teens
By Pastor Joel Stockstill

In a day where wickedness and violence abound toward a generation, the lost art of deliverance is needed more than ever before. When Pharaoh enslaved a generation of God's people, Moses was sent to deliver them from slavery and lead them to the Promised Land of God's rest. Today is a similar day where the Lord is raising up leaders who will obey his voice to deliver a generation that has been attacked and enslaved to the bondages of sin. Aurora Wells is a voice in the wilderness crying out for such deliverance. The Lord has stirred in her heart a message of freedom and release for this generation of hurting young people. As you read this book I pray that the Lord would quicken in your spirit the great need that exists for people of deliverance ministry and the burden to step out and bring freedom to a hurting generation.

Prayers that Bring Deliverance for Teens

By Aurora Wells

Copyright © 2012 by Aurora Wells

Prayers that Bring Deliverance for Teens
by Aurora Wells

Printed in the United States of America

ISBN 9781624196690

All rights reserved solely by the author. The author guarantees all contents are original and do not infringe upon the legal rights of any other person or work. No part of this book may be reproduced in any form without the permission of the author. The views expressed in this book are not necessarily those of the publisher.

Unless otherwise indicated, Bible quotations are taken from the King James Version of the Bible.

www.xulonpress.com

Acknowledgements

First and foremost I acknowledge my Heavenly Father for giving me the inspiration to put these prayers in print so that others can experience the same glorious deliverance you have worked in my life. I can't live without you!

To my husband Hilton, I consider myself blessed by God to have privileged me to marry a man like you. Thank you for challenging me to complete this project.

To my awesomely anointed children, you bring a continual flow of joy to my life.

Thank you mom, dad and all of my family for your love, prayers and support.

To Pastors Carl and Jeanette Clark, thank you for your prayers, covering and impartation.

To the Rivers of Living Water Church family, you are an awesome group of people. Thank you for all that you do for us! It is a privilege to serve you. "We're going somewhere!"

To Mimi (Rosalee Davis), Evangelist Barbara Baker and the entire First Church of God in Christ family, thank you all. There is no way I can describe the impact you all had on me. Everything I do for

Christ is built on the foundation that you laid.

To all the intercessors that God has blessed me to partner with, thank you for your impartation.

I would like to thank Allison, my editor, for your kind and encouraging words. You were the first person to read this book in its entirety and your heartfelt response let me know that this book was ready to be released to the world.

Last but not least I would like to thank Kaelyn Smith. Your passion for God inspired me to create a handbook that would equip young people to effectively war in the spirit.

Table of Contents

Introduction	xi
Salvation	14
Confession	15
Morning Prayer	17
Abandonment	19
Abortion, the effects of	21
Abuse	23
Addiction	25
Anger	27
Compromise	29
Depression	32
Eating Disorders (anorexia, bulimia)	35
Father Wounds	37
Fear	40
Gluttony	42
Gossip	44
Greed/Materialism	46
Guilt	48
Homosexuality	50
Jealousy	53
Laziness	55
Low Self-Esteem	57
Lust	59

Prayers that Bring Deliverance for Teens

Mental Illness	61
Mother Wound	63
Offense	66
Pornography	68
Poverty	70
Pride	73
Rebellion	75
Religion	77
Self-Mutilation	80
Soul-Ties	82
Suicide	85
Witchcraft/Occult	87

Introduction

I wrote this book out of a strong burden and desire to help young people be set free from the bondages of Satan. Many young people love God and desire with all of their hearts to live for God, but they continue to struggle with bondages, addictions, and hurts from the past. Satan uses these issues to hinder, delay, or destroy the lives of countless individuals, who would otherwise be a mighty weapon in the hand of God.

Although the evil works of Satan are not only confined to the younger generation, there are issues that are specific to this generation. This book targets issues such as depression, self-mutilation, pornography, low self-esteem, and many other relevant concerns that plague today's youth.

>There is hope for this generation!
>There is freedom!
>There is deliverance, and it is only found in Jesus!

The Book of 1 John 3:8 declares that Jesus came to destroy the works of the devil, and he proved this throughout the gospels when He healed the sick and cast out the demons, he states, "And these signs shall follow them that believe; In my name they shall cast out devils. . . ." (Mark 16:17). You don't have to be a preacher, pastor, or even and apostle. All you have to do is believe.

This book is constructed as a resource manual full of powerful prayers that boldly confront the forces of darkness at work in your life. Each topic is easily referenced and can be prayed on a daily basis. Feel free to repeat the prayers as long as necessary until the words become alive in your heart and you begin to experience deliverance. The prayers can be adjusted to confessions. For example, instead of saying, "Father, I ask you to forgive me," you would say, "Father, I thank you for forgiving me," and so on with each prayer.

These prayers can also be used as a tool of intercession. A friend, parent, or concerned loved one can pray these prayers on behalf of someone who is bound but does not have a desire to seek God in prayer. Simply replace the word "I" with the individual's name and watch God begin to work. These prayers are constructed in a general pattern of confession, repentance, renunciation, and praise.

These are some of the terms that you will encounter in many of the prayers as defined by Webster's Dictionary:

> Deliver: 1. to set free : rescue from actual or feared evil : SAVE
> Confess: 1. to tell or make known (as something wrong or damaging to oneself)
> Repent: 1: to turn from sin and resolve to reform one's life
> Bind: 2: to restrain as if by tying

Introduction

> Command: 1: to direct authoritatively : ORDER
>
> Renounce: 1: to give up, refuse, or resign usually by formal declaration.
>
> 2: To refuse to further follow, obey, or recognize
>
> Declare: 1: to make known formally, officially, or explicitly: ANNOUNCE
>
> 2. to state emphatically : AFFIRM

Deliverance is available to you. Do you want it? Are you willing to surrender yourself to God and make adjustments to your life to maintain it? Are you tired of suffering defeat and ready to take a bold stand against the enemy of your soul? If the answer is yes and you dare to continue, turn the page and locate the specific area in which you seek deliverance. When you pray, pray with boldness knowing that God is on your side and desires to see you set free! Pray in faith knowing that your words are not falling to the ground, but they are working in the unseen realm of the spirit bringing about change and deliverance into your life!

Get ready to be set free and walk in the abundant life that Jesus came for you to live!

Salvation

If you would like to know Jesus Christ as your savior, just say this prayer: "Lord, I realize that I am a sinner. I believe you sent your son Jesus to save me from sin and from hell. I ask you to forgive me of all my sins, come into my heart, and help me live a life that reflects the gratitude that I have in my heart for what you have done for me. I confess that today I am saved, and I am now a child of God.

In Jesus' name, amen!

Scripture References
John 3:16, Romans 10:9-10

Confession

I declare that I am a child of the living God. I am the head and not the tail. I am above only and not beneath. I am a member of a chosen generation, a royal priesthood, a holy nation, one of God's special people called to proclaim the praises of Him who called me out of darkness into His marvelous light. I know that I can do all things through Christ that strengthens me. I know that my God shall supply all of my needs according to His riches in glory by Christ Jesus. I understand that greater is He that is in me, than he that is in the world, and whenever the enemy comes in like a flood the Spirit of the Lord will lift up a standard against Him. I will endure hardship as a good soldier of Jesus Christ, for in all things I am more than a conqueror through Him that loves me. My God has not given me a spirit of fear, but of power, love, and a sound mind. I will let no man despise my youth, but I will be an example to all believers in word, conduct, love, spirit, faith, and purity.

In Jesus' name, amen!

Scripture references
Deuteronomy 28:13, 1 Peter 2:9, Philippians 4:13,

Philippians 4:19, 1 John 4:4, Isaiah 59:19, Romans 8:37, 2 Timothy 1:7, 1 Timothy 4:12

Morning Prayer

This is the day that the Lord has made, and I will rejoice and be glad in it. Father, I thank you for keeping me from all hurt, harm, and danger, as I slept in the comfort of your protection. Thank you for the dreams you allowed me to experience. I pray that you will reveal to me their hidden meanings and messages, and remind me to pray for those I dreamt about.

Now, Father, I speak to my day and declare that I walk in purpose and destiny. I thank you that my footsteps are ordered by you, as you lead me in paths of righteousness. When I am tempted by the evil one, you provide me with a way of escape.

I declare that my spiritual ears are open to hear your voice as I go throughout my day. My spiritual eyes are focused and keen, and I am able to discern good from evil. I bind every trick, plan, and plot of the enemy against my life. I bind every incident and accident and declare that no weapon that is formed against me shall be able to prosper, and every tongue that rises against me in judgment I will condemn.

I commit myself to walk in the spirit, so that I won't fulfill the lusts of my flesh. I put on the whole armor of God, so I can stand firm. I put on the garment of praise and cast off the spirit of heaviness, and declare that the joy of the Lord is my strength.

I yield myself to the Holy Spirit and commit myself to operate in love, joy, peace, patience, kindness, goodness, faithfulness, gentleness, and self-control. I forgive all those who would hurt or offend me in advance, and I'm determined to walk in love in every situation. I declare that the favor of the Lord goes before me like a shield.

I pray that you allow me to discern the opportunities that you give me to share the gospel and be a witness for you.

I thank you that you have not given me a spirit of fear, but you have given me power, love, and a sound mind. I have no reason to fear or worry, for you promised that you would never leave or forsake me and you will be with me always. Therefore, I face this day that you have given me with boldness, faith, expectancy, and great excitement. I declare that I am blessed, my home is blessed, my school is blessed, and my job is blessed. Today, I place myself in our hands. Use me as an instrument to advance your kingdom and bring you glory.

In Jesus' name, amen!

Scripture references
Psalm 118:24, Numbers 12:6, Psalm 37:23, Psalm 23:3, 1 Corinthians 10:13, Isaiah 54:17, Galatians 5:16, Isaiah 61:3, Nehemiah 8:10, Galatians 5:22, Psalm 5:12, 2 Timothy 1:7, Deuteronomy 31:6

Abandonment

Father, I come to you today for deliverance from abandonment. Lord, I thank you that you are the healer of broken hearts. You restore and redeem broken lives. Since I have experienced rejection and abandonment in the past, I lay my life in your hands and trust you to heal me and make me whole. Father, I have allowed my past experiences to determine the way I view myself and my relationships with others. Since the people I trusted the most, who were supposed to love me and take care of me, have abandoned or neglected me, I have begun to feel alone and unwanted. Even when people come into my life, who truly want to love and embrace me, I have a hard time receiving their love, because I expect them to leave me just like the others did. Even though I am surrounded by other people, I find myself living my life this way.

I want to be free to receive your love and the love of the people you have placed in my life. I realize that my trust and confidence is in you, and although people may come and go, your love and protection remains constant. You promised that you would never leave me or forsake me. Even when my mother and father have forsaken me, you said you would take me up. You have adopted me and made me a member of your own household. Your word says that you set lonely people in families so I thank you for sending Godly people into my life who will love and embrace me.

I thank you, Father, for healing my heart and making me whole. I will seek you daily in prayer, worship, and studying of the word so that my faith and trust in you will increase.

Right now, in the name of Jesus, I command the spirit of abandonment to leave me. I am no longer in agreement with abandonment's lies. I am loveable. Many people love and care for me. But more importantly, God loves me. God's love is greater than the love of any mother, father, sister, brother, or friend. His love alone makes me whole and complete. I declare today that I am free from the spirit of abandonment. Lord, I give you praise and glory for my deliverance.

In Jesus' name, amen!

Scripture references
Psalm 103:17, Deuteronomy 31:6, Psalm 27:10, Psalm 68:6, John 15:13

The Effects of Abortion

Father, in the name of Jesus I come to you today for deliverance and healing from the effects of abortion. Lord, my heart is broken over the sin of abortion. I acknowledge that the child I aborted was not just a lifeless lump of tissue and flesh, but was an innocent, unborn person, who was created in the image of God with purpose and destiny. Father, forgive me for killing my child. Forgive me for taking a life that I did not create. I receive your forgiveness. Since you have forgiven me, I now am free to forgive myself. I will no longer walk in condemnation over this sin. All regret, shame, grief, sorrow, and mourning are removed from me today. Jesus Christ the Son of God has set me free; therefore, I am free indeed. God does not condemn me; therefore, I will not condemn myself. Satan has no right to accuse me, because God has removed my sin from me as far as the east is from the west.

I not only forgive myself, but I forgive every individual involved in my decision process and those who performed the abortion.

Today I remove from my possession all items or artifacts that I have held onto that bring on feelings of sorrow and condemnation. I am free to love and celebrate my child, and I pray that one day I will be able to meet him or her in Heaven.

I declare today that I am free. I will never again walk in guilt and shame from the past. I am forgiven. I have a spirit of praise and thanksgiving. My future is bright, and I am walking in purpose and destiny every day.

In Jesus' name, amen!

Scripture references
1 John 1:9, Exodus 20:13, Romans 8:1, John 8:36, Ephesians 4:32, 1 Corinthians 15:33, Ephesians 5:11, 2 Corinthians 6:17

Abuse
(pray in conjunction with Offense)

Father, in the name of Jesus, I come to you today for deliverance from abuse. I am currently being or have been _____(name abuse) by _____(abuser's name). I know this is not what you desire for me. I realize that Satan is the source of evil; therefore, I bind the work of Satan against me that is operating through _____(abuser's name). I declare that I belong to God, and Satan has no right to hurt me. I plead the blood of Jesus over myself, and I ask Jesus to deliver me from this situation. Touch _____ (abuser's name) and give them a heart of repentance. Give me the strength to stand up to them and put an end to this abuse. Give me wisdom and show me who I can confide in to help me out of this situation.

Father, I ask you to heal me of the effects of this abuse. Cleanse my heart, my mind, and my body of all perversion. Change the way I think. Help me not to live life as a victim but as an overcomer in Christ Jesus. Help me to forgive _____ (abuser's name) and trust you to bring punishment on those who hurt me. Vengeance is your job; there-

Prayers that Bring Deliverance for Teens

fore, I will not try to get _____(abuser's name) back for hurting me. Help me to forgive those who should have helped me but didn't.

I break the cycle of abuse in my life in the name of Jesus. I will not be drawn into abusive relationships, but I have wisdom and discernment to know which people are healthy for me to connect with. I will not draw abuse to myself. The mark the abuse left upon my life is erased by the blood of Jesus, and every void and empty place is filled up with the love of God. I am a new creature in Christ, and abuse does not define who I am or how God can use me. I submit my life to God for Him to use me as an awesome testimony of how God delivers and heals broken hearts and lives. All shame, blame, and guilt are removed, and I am free, free, free!

In Jesus' name, amen!

Scripture references
John 10:10, Romans 12:19, Exodus 15:26, 2 Corinthians 5:17, Ephesians 4:32

Addiction

Father I come to you today for deliverance from an addiction to _____(name addiction). I willfully admit that I am addicted to _____. Father, I ask you to forgive me for allowing myself to become addicted. I realize that it is a sin for me to allow something other than your Holy Spirit to control me. Today I am fed up and disgusted with _____, and I am determined to walk in freedom from this addiction that is destroying my life.

Father, I ask you to heal me of any pain that I have been trying to medicate with this addiction (confess it here). I lay every hurtful and painful experience before you, and I ask you wash me in your blood and remove the pain.

Father, I ask that you would supernaturally detoxify my body and remove the craving and desire for _____ from me.

Today I disassociate myself from every person, place, or thing that would tempt me back into sin. I sever all ties with friends and associates who would tempt me to sin. I separate myself from parties, hangouts, groups, and associations that endorse substance use and abuse. Today I humble myself and I willfully make a decision to be held accountable by a parent, pastor, or mentor.

Spirit of addiction, I command you to leave my life, I am no longer under your influence or control. I am covered in the blood of Jesus, and I choose to walk in victory. I close the doors that allowed you in through unresolved issues and the undisciplined areas of my flesh.

Today I declare that I am free never to be bound again!

In Jesus' name, amen!

Scripture references
1 John 1:9, Ephesians 5:18, Hebrews 9:14, 2 Corinthians 6:17, 1 Corinthians 15:33, 2 Corinthians 6:17, Ephesians 5:11

Anger/Violence

Father, in the name of Jesus I come to you today for deliverance from anger. Father, forgive me for allowing anger to rule in my life. Your word says to be angry but to not allow that anger to cause me to sin. My anger has led me to do and say things that sometimes hurt others and even myself. Your word also says not to let the sun go down on my wrath, but at times I find myself angry over long periods of time, and I have a hard time letting go of and resolving my anger. Father, I thank you for forgiving me, and I ask you to heal my heart of deep-rooted issues that cause me to be angry. I release all the pain from my past—all hurt, abuse, and offense. I forgive all the people who have hurt me, because in Christ God has forgiven me.

Father, I ask you to strengthen me in my inner man/woman, so that I will be able to discipline my emotions against anger. I realize that my anger does not produce the righteous results that I really desire, but only makes situations worse. By faith I declare that I walk in self-control and patience with myself and others. Spirit of anger, I command you to lose your hold and come out of me in the name of Jesus. Generational anger, I declare that your influence stops here. By the power of God at work in me, I will no longer yield to the temptation to become angry, enraged, or violent. I command the spirit of violence to come out of me now in the name of Jesus. I am no longer in agreement with Satan or my flesh. I will no longer use anger and violence as a form of manipulation, domination, or control over others to get my way. My flesh is now under the control of my spirit and will no longer cause me to sin.

Today I remove from my possession all music, movies, video games, books, magazines, or any other form of media that would cause a spirit of anger or violence to rise up in me. I remove myself from all associations with people, groups, or organizations that would tempt me to fall back into the bondage of anger and violence. Right now, I declare that I am free from the control of anger and violence. My emotions are under control, and you are teaching me daily to properly deal with my feelings and to handle my life situations in a way that expresses the love, peace, and joy of God that is inside of me. All glory, honor and praise belong to you, Father.

In Jesus' name, amen!

Scripture references
1 John 1:9, Ephesians 4:26, Hebrews 12:15, Ephesians 4:32, Ephesians 3:16, James 1:26, Ephesians 4:2, Galatians 5:16, 2 Corinthians 6:17, 1 Corinthians 15:33, 2 Corinthians 6:17, Ephesians 5:11

Compromise

Father, I come to you today for deliverance from a spirit of compromise. First of all, Father, I thank you for saving me and giving me a desire to live for you. Thank you for calling me by name and allowing me to be an ambassador for you. Now Father, I ask you to forgive me for compromising my beliefs, convictions, and my testimony. Even though I desire to live for you, I find myself saying, doing, or being things that are not in agreement with who I really am. Sometimes I just want to fit in and be accepted by those around me, and I tend to take the easy way out instead of standing for what is right.

God, I ask you to give me strength to stand firm in my convictions regardless of the pressure I feel around me. Make me like Shadrach, Meshach, and Abednego, who were able to look death in the face, because they were willing to face persecution rather than compromise and bow down to worship idols. They were not afraid of man, who is only able to hurt the body, but they honored God, who is lord over all. Give me the boldness that these men had so that I can be a light to my generation. I will be bold and let my light shine, for a light that is hidden can draw no one to Christ. I will not hide my light by laughing at impure jokes, watching impure movies, taking part in conversations that tear down instead of buildup, by wearing clothing just to get attention or fit in. By displaying attitudes that do not reflect the joy, love, and purity of Christ, or any other action or attitude that is contrary to the new nature that Christ has placed in me.

In Jesus' name I bind and cast out the spirit of compromise and any other spirits that promote compromise such as people pleasing, fear of man, _____(name any others).

I declare that I am free to be the light of the world, the salt of the earth, and an ambassador for Christ. I make decisions based on the conviction of the Holy Spirit inside of me. I do not have an unhealthy desire to be accepted by others because I know I am accepted by God.

I remove from my possession every movie, CD, article of clothing, book, magazine, or any other item that goes against my convictions. I remove myself from all people and groups _____(name them) that do not respect my convictions and try to pressure me into doing things that I don't really want to do. They are not truly friends. God, I ask you to introduce me to people who will encourage me and respect my faith and my God. God, I thank you for setting me free. I am walking in victory and liberty from this day forward.

In Jesus' name, amen!

Scripture references
1 John 1:9, 2 Thessalonians 2:15, James 1:6, Daniel 3, Matthew 5:16, Matthew 10:28, Ephesians 1:6, 1 Corinthians 15:33, 2 Corinthians 6:17, Ephesians 5:11

Depression

Father, in the name of Jesus I bind the spirit of depression that has taken over or is attempting to take ahold of my life. First of all, I come out of agreement with every lie of hopelessness and despair that the enemy has spoken to me. The truth that I know will set me free. I come out of agreement with the idea that my life or situation is hopeless and will never get better. The truth is that your thoughts toward me are of peace and not evil, which give me a future and hope. I purge my mind of every thought that the enemy sent my way. Forgive me, Lord, for not holding to the truth of your word. Forgive me for focusing all of my attention on myself, my issues, my problems, my situation, and my inadequacies. I determine today to set my mind on things that are true, noble, right, pure, lovely, admirable, excellent, or praiseworthy. My mind is no longer working against me, because I am taking every thought captive, and if it does not line up with these criteria I will reject it immediately and will not allow it to take root.

Father, forgive me for not walking in a spirit of praise and thanksgiving. Forgive me for being more consumed with what is wrong than with all of the

Depression

goodness, mercy, and favor you continue to show me. I declare today that I will not forget all of your benefits, but I am mindful of the fact that you forgive all my sins and heal all my diseases. You redeem my life from the pit and crown me with love and compassion. You satisfy my desires with good things so that my youth is renewed like the eagles. I determine today to walk by faith and not by sight; therefore, I will give thanks to the Lord and His praise will always be on my lips. I release an exuberant praise. A praise that will release the chains of oppression and depression and bring total and complete breakthrough in my life.

Today I will remove from my life every item, possession, or association that initiates lowness, oppression or depression. Any music or movies that nurse or encourage a spirit of depression I remove from my possession today. Any items, artifacts, or pictures that bring on feelings of sorrow or depression I remove from my possession today. Today I sever all relationships with people, places, groups, or associations that initiate or encourage darkness or depression. I am no longer in darkness, but I have been translated into the kingdom of God, which is light. I break every covenant or agreement that I made knowingly or unknowingly with Satan and his kingdom of darkness through movies, music, art, or any other form that promoted witchcraft or sorcery of any kind. Satan, I renounce you and your kingdom, and you are defeated in my life. I declare that the light of the glory of God is infiltrating every area of my body, soul, and spirit, and today Satan is displaced and removed never to return again. I speak to my body to be strengthened and renewed from all the negative, life-draining effects that depression had on my body. I declare that my joy is restored, and the joy of the Lord has become my strength. Weariness and fatigue have to leave my body, because the Holy Spirit is quickening my body right now. I declare that Jesus is Lord and the Holy Spirit lives in me in power and might, and today I declare I am free of every form of depression, oppression, lowness, and suicide.

In Jesus' name, amen!

Scripture references
1 John 1:9, John 8:44, Jeremiah 29:11, Philippians 4:8, 2 Corinthians 10:5, Psalm 103:1-3, Acts 16:25-26, 1 Corinthians 15:33, Ephesians 5:11,
2 Corinthians 6:17, Colossians 1:13, Acts 26:18, Nehemiah 8:10, Romans 8:11

Eating Disorders
(Bulimia, Anorexia)

Father, in the name of Jesus I pray for deliverance from eating disorders such as Anorexia and Bulimia. First of all, Father, I ask you to forgive me for allowing my relationship with food and eating to become out of balance. I also ask you to forgive me for allowing my body image to become an idol. You said not to have any other god before you, and I have allowed my body to become so important that I was willing to jeopardize my health and my convictions just to obtain what the world told me was desirable. I ask you to heal me of every negative word and message that told me I am not acceptable unless I look a certain way. Reveal to me your love and acceptance, and let me see myself the way you see me.

Today I renounce every unhealthy eating habit and disorder and acknowledge my past actions as sinful. I command the demonic spirits that influence me in this area to come out of me now in the name of Jesus. I am no longer in agreement with you. I don't believe the lies that you have been speaking to me. I am free from your influence and control. I declare that I am no longer bulimic or anorexic. I

Prayers that Bring Deliverance for Teens

am not afraid of food or eating. I am free to eat and enjoy food in a healthy, balanced manner. I sever ties and associations with people who would tempt me to reenter that bondage. I rid myself of all magazines, books, or clothing that would cause me to have unrealistic desires for my body. I declare that my body is beautiful. I love my body, every inch and imperfection. I am blessed to have limbs, hips, thighs, and arms. My body is the temple of the Holy Ghost. A vessel for God to use in this earth to carry out His work and bring Him glory. Nothing more, nothing less. I will not exalt my body for my own selfish gain. I will not allow it to be my source of self-worth, acceptance, and confidence. Since God loves and accepts me unconditionally, I will love and accept myself unconditionally.

In Jesus' name, amen!

Scripture references
1 John 1:9, Exodus 20:1-5, Psalm 139:14, 1 Corinthians 6:19, Ephesians 5:11,
2 Corinthians 6:19, 1 Corinthians 15:33

Father Wounds

Father, today in the name of Jesus I come to you for healing and deliverance for the wounds I received from my natural father. Father, I confess to you that my heart and soul have been wounded by my father. I know that you are the God of all comfort and the mender of broken hearts; therefore, I open mine up to you and ask you to heal me, mend me, and make me whole. Heal me of all abuse and injustice my father has inflicted upon me. Wash away abusive words spoken in anger or rage. Replace them with your words of peace and loving kindness. Wash away words he spoke to me out of disappointment or disapproval. Replace them with words of approval and acceptance. Wash away the imprint left on my identity with hurtful or humiliating nicknames and replace them with your words of affirmation and identity. Heal me of the physical abuse he inflicted upon me. Heal my mind and remove the fear and timidity he instilled in me through his domineering or violent actions.

Fill the empty place he left in my heart by not being involved in my life. Bring peace to my mind that has been trying to understand why he left me or just was not interested in me.

Prayers that Bring Deliverance for Teens

Father, today I commit all these hurtful memories and experiences to you. I realize that I cannot compare you with my natural father, who hurt and disappointed me. You are perfect and full of love and compassion. Therefore, I trust you with my heart and life. You said that when mother and father forsake me you would take me in. You said you are a father to the orphan; therefore, I trust you to fill the void that my father left empty. Expose any unhealthy relationships that I am trying to use to fill the void my father left through a lack of affection, approval, or presence in my life. Help me to seek you for complete healing and fulfillment.

Father, today I make the decision to forgive my father. He is wrong for what he did, but I no longer hold his faults against him. Help me to see him for what he is: a soul that needs Jesus, who has experienced his own share of hurt and disappointment. Give me a heart of mercy and compassion for him. You instructed us to forgive others just as God through Christ has forgiven us; therefore, I forgive my father because you have forgiven me. Lord, help me to sort through all the negative emotions associated with my father. I realize that complete healing is a process and will take time, but I will trust you every step of the way. I lay aside all hatred, anger, resentment, bitterness, and any other negative emotion I have held toward him. I do not look to him for an apology or repayment for the wrongs he has committed against me. Lord, I look to you to restore to me what was taken or neglected.

Father, I ask you to bring about restoration with my father. Help me to be obedient when you give me instructions. Give me words to say and actions to take for this God-ordained relationship to be restored. If my father is deceased, help me find closure even though he is no longer with me.

Today I declare that I am healed, healthy, and whole. I am loved immensely by my Father in Heaven.

In Jesus' name, amen!

Scripture references
2 Corinthians 1:3-4, 2 Timothy 1:7, Romans 8:15, Psalms 27:10, Ephesians 4:32, Ecclesiastes 3:1-2

Fear

Father, right now in the name of Jesus I break the spirit of fear from my life. Today I make the decision to use my faith to believe the promises you made in your word rather than the lies the enemy has spoken to me. Lord, you are my light and my salvation, so who shall I fear? You are the stronghold of my life, so of whom shall I be afraid? I don't fear my enemies, because when they try to attack me you said they would stumble and fall. If you are for me, who can be against me? I don't fear a day of trouble and disaster, for you said you would keep me safe in your dwelling, hide me in your shelter, and lift me high upon a rock. You said no harm would befall me, and no disaster would come near my tent, because you would command your angels to guard me in all my ways. I don't fear the terror of night or the dangers of the day. I don't fear the opinions of men, who can only harm the body, but I honor and respect God's opinion of me. I don't fear sickness, disease, or pestilence, because you said that a thousand may fall at my side, and ten thousand at my right hand, but it will not come near me (Psalm 91). You promised to forgive all my sins and heal all my disease. I don't fear death, because Jesus has conquered the grave. As a believer, to die and to be absent from the body is only a promotion to being present with the Lord.

Today I remove from my possession all movies, books, magazines, pictures and music that promote a spirit of fear.

I declare today that I am totally and completely free from the torment of fear. I am no longer in agreement with the spirit of fear, and I command it to leave my mind, my body, and my home. I set my mind upon the Word of God. Every time a lie comes to my mind that causes fear in my heart, I will open my mouth and declare God's words. All anxiety, tension, and uneasiness are removed, because my heart is trusting safely in the Lord. Thank you lord, for I called upon you and you delivered me from all my fears.

In Jesus' name, amen!

Scripture references
John 8:44, Psalm 91, Psalm 103:3, Revelations 1:18, 2 Corinthians 5:6-7,
2 Timothy 1:7, 1 John 4:18, Philippians 4:6, 1 Corinthians 15:33, Ephesians 5:11, 2 Corinthians 6:17

Gluttony

Father, in the name of Jesus, I pray for deliverance from gluttony. I ask you to forgive me for allowing food to become an idol in my life. Your word says that whatever I submit myself to I become its slave. I have submitted to my appetite and therefore become a slave to food. I have used food as a source of comfort when I was feeling emotional unrest, a source of satisfaction when my soul was feeling empty and really longing for you. But today, in the name of Jesus, I break the power of food over my life.

I cast out the spirit of gluttony in the name of Jesus. I will not be controlled by the unquenchable appetite of my flesh. I come out of agreement with every negative confession I have made about myself concerning food. I no longer "love food," but I enjoy the food God has blessed me with, and I receive it with a thankful attitude. I will no longer say "I can't help myself," but I declare that I operate in self-control and discipline over my flesh. I no longer turn to food for comfort and satisfaction, but I find my delight in you and fulfilling your purposes in my life. I sever associations that would tempt me to operate in gluttony. I remove all items from my possession that would help nurture and promote this sin. Instead of fantasizing about food, I will meditate on your word, for your word is more satisfying than my daily food. I am free to enjoy food as a blessing from God without overindulgence.

In Jesus' name, amen!

Scripture references
1 John 1:9, Romans 6:19, Matthew 4:4, Proverbs 18:21, Proverbs 23:21, Job 23:12

Gossip

Father, in the name of Jesus, I come to you today for deliverance from gossip. Father, first I ask you to forgive me for gossiping. I realize that gossip is a work of the flesh and is not pleasing to you. My gossiping has hurt people that I care for and even those I don't know. Gossip has hurt and even destroyed relationships that were very important to me. Today I confess the sin of gossip, and I make a new commitment to crucify my flesh and take back control of my tongue. I ask your Holy Spirit to guide my tongue and bring conviction to my heart every time I get ready to release gossip. I don't have to carry the latest news. People enjoy me for who I am. Let the words that I speak be gracious and build up the people I am talking to and about and not tear them down. Help me to hold my tongue when I am tempted to spread other people's business even when it is true.

I cast out the spirit of gossip that has been using me as a vessel to tear others down. I am no longer in agreement with you, and I declare that I am a vessel for the Holy Spirit. I separate myself from all people and groups that promote and encourage gossip. I remove from my possession all personal notes, letters, magazines, and any other source of media that contains gossip.

Today I am free from gossip!
In Jesus' name, amen!

Scripture references
1 John 1:9, Proverbs 11:13, Proverbs 16:28, Colossians 4:6

Greed/Materialism

Father, today in the name of Jesus I come to you for deliverance from greed and materialism. First of all, I ask you Lord to forgive me for seeking and lusting after material things more than seeking you. I ask you to heal the broken and empty places in me that I have been trying to fill by acquiring things. I realize now that no matter how much stuff I obtain, I will always be longing for more. Help me to seek you first with all my heart, and to trust you to add any material possession that I may need or want.

Lord, forgive me for using possessions as a way of proving that I belong or that I am superior to others. Underneath all the stuff lies an emptiness that only you can truly fill. Lord, let me see who I am in you. Help me study your word and spend time in your presence, so that I can find my true identity. I am a child of the Most High God, dearly loved and cared for by Him. He knows me deeply and intimately, and loves me for who I really am.

Father, let me direct the same tenacity and determination that I used to gain material goods to do my part in advancing your kingdom and spreading your gospel throughout the earth.

Greed/materialism

Today I renounce greed and materialism. I command greed and materialism to leave me now in the name of Jesus. You have distracted me from God's purpose for long enough. I declare that I am a giver, and I do not hoard my possessions, but I use them to bring glory to God and share with others. I remove from my possession every book, magazine, movie, TV show, poster, artwork, article of clothing, jewelry, or any other item that promotes or endorses greed and materialism. I separate myself from every person, group, club, organization, and individual that promotes greed and materialism.

Today I declare that I am free. I give freely, and the giving nature of Jesus Christ is displayed throughout my life.

In Jesus' name, amen!

Scripture references
1 John 1:9, Matthew 6:33, Luke 12:15, Colossians 3:5, Romans 12:13, Acts 20:35, 1 Corinthians 15:33, 2 Corinthians, 6:17, Ephesians 5:11

Guilt

Father, I come to you today for deliverance from guilt. First of all, I thank you for sending your son Jesus to die on the cross. He paid the price for the sins of all mankind; therefore, we are no longer guilty but innocent when we put our faith in Him and receive his forgiveness. Now Father, I confess all sin to you, and by faith I receive your forgiveness. I confess the specific sin of _____ that has been causing me to feel guilt and separation from your presence. When I confess my sins, you are faithful and just to forgive me and cleanse me of all unrighteousness. By faith I receive not only your forgiveness but your cleansing.

Right now I declare that I am free from guilt, and I have the right to come boldly into the presence of my Father. I live by faith in God's word and not by how I feel; therefore, even though I may still feel guilty, the blood of Jesus has made me innocent. I command guilt to leave me now in the name of Jesus. I will no longer dwell on past sins or mistakes that make me feel guilty, but I dwell on the word of God. His word says that there is no condemnation for those who are in Christ Jesus. He, who the Son set free, is free indeed. Christ has set me free; therefore, I am free indeed. The blood of Jesus is able to cleanse me of a guilty conscience. Psalms 103:12 says that God removes my sins as far as the east is from the west. Since God does not hold my sins against me and forgets them all together, then I will do the same.

God, I praise you for setting me free and renewing my mind. You are an awesome God, and I will continually praise you for your love and forgiveness.

In Jesus' name, amen!

Scripture references
Hebrews 9:14, 1 John 1:9, Hebrews 4:6, Galatians 3:11, John 8:36, Romans 8:1

Homosexuality

Father, in the name of Jesus I pray for deliverance from homosexuality. First of all, I ask you to forgive me for the sins I have committed physically and mentally. I acknowledge that same-sex attraction is not from God, and it is the perversion of the wonderful gift of sexuality that you have given mankind. Now, Father, I ask you to heal me of all the experiences and encounters that have taken place in my life that led me into homosexuality. Father, heal my heart of all abuse—physical, sexual, verbal, emotional, and neglect that caused me to be vulnerable to homosexuality. I forgive all the individuals and the gender of those who abused me.

Father, I ask you to wash my mind of images I have seen that planted a seed and sparked an interest in same-sex relationships. Father, I ask you to help me renew my mind concerning the gender you created me to be. You created me—male/female—and you did not make a mistake. I reject the lie of the enemy who tries to convince me that I am really a man/woman trapped in a male/female body.

Father, heal me of the insecurity I have felt concerning my manhood/womanhood, and when I may

Homosexuality

have felt that I didn't measure up as a man/woman. I will not allow society or culture to tell me that I am less of a man/woman, because I do not fit a certain mold. I am confident in the fact that I have been fearfully and wonderfully made by You.

Today I set myself in agreement with God's word and His will for my life. I commit myself to renew my mind by meditating on the Word of God. Every thought that would promote same-sex relationships I will take hold of it and cast it down and out of my thinking. I will discipline my thoughts and not allow sexual fantasizing.

Today I renounce homosexuality and everything associated with its lifestyle. I sever every relationship that would promote or nurture homosexuality. I disassociate myself from every group, social club, Internet blog, and every other social connection that would temp me to sin. Today I remove every book, magazine, movie, TV show, poster, artwork, article of clothing, jewelry, and any other item that would connect me mentally, emotionally, or physically or socially with the homosexual lifestyle.

I take authority over my body and declare that I will not burn with lust in my sexual organs. My body chemistry is being washed and renewed and set back to its original setting to desire the opposite sex.

Right now I plead the blood of Jesus over myself, and I command the spirit of lesbianism or homosexuality to come out of me now in the name of Jesus. I am no longer in agreement with homosexuality. I do not want its presence and influence in my life any longer.

Prayers that Bring Deliverance for Teens

Today I declare that I am free from homosexuality, lesbianism, and/or bisexuality. By the authority of God's word, I am a new creature, and everything related to the sinful nature of homosexuality has passed away. I do not walk in guilt and shame. The light of the glory of God is shining within me, and the darkness is not able to remain in its presence. Father, use my life as a testimony to help set others free. Today Jesus has set me free, and I am free indeed.

In Jesus' name, amen!

Scripture references
1 John 1:9, Leviticus 18:22, Ephesians 4:32, Romans 12:2, Genesis 1:27, John 8:44, Psalm 139:14, 2 Corinthians 10:5, 1 Corinthians 15:33, Ephesians 5:11, 2 Corinthians 6:17

Jealousy

Father, I come to you today for deliverance from jealousy. I ask you God to forgive me for focusing on what you have given to others without acknowledging your blessing in my own life.

I have not been able to celebrate the success and gifts of others, because their success and gifts make me feel as though they are better than me. I realize today that this is a lie from Satan. He wants me to be so consumed with what others have that I don't focus on and develop the gifts and abilities you have given me. You want to use me to help advance your work on Earth, and you have given me unique gifts and abilities to fulfill your plan. Lord, show me the gifts you have given me. Show me how you want to use me and how I can help others. Help me understand how perfectly you have designed me, how I am fearfully and wonderfully made. How I am known by the God of the Universe, The Creator of Heaven and Earth. Help me not to compare myself with other people.

What I am or what I have does not make me any better or any less than anyone else on Earth. God does not show respect to people based on their status

Prayers that Bring Deliverance for Teens

and ability. The rich and poor have this in common; the Lord is the maker of them both. I realize that every person on Earth can only have what has been delegated to him by God. God, you determined what I have and what I will not have, and I am thankful to you for both. I see all people equally as you see them, whether they are TV stars or homeless on the street. My worth is not determined by what I have, who my friends are, my physical appearance, or abilities. My worth comes only from the fact that I am known by the Almighty God. I have been created in His image with destiny and purpose. I am loved by my Father with unending, unconditional love, and I am the apple of His eye. He has a customized plan for my life that is unlike anyone before or after me, and He has given me everything I need to fulfill His purpose.

In the name of Jesus, I command every foul spirit that would tempt me to be jealous of others to leave me now. I sever all relationships with people who put me down or encourage the spirit of jealousy. I rid myself of all books, magazines, movies, TV shows, pictures, and music that would nurture jealousy in my heart. I declare today that I am free from jealousy, and I am able to enjoy the gifts and success of others. I thank you, Father, for freedom today.
In Jesus' name, amen!

Scripture references
1 John 1:9, 2 Corinthians 10:12, Ephesians 4:7, Psalm 139:14, Luke 12:15, Proverbs 22:2, Acts 10:34, 1 Corinthians 15:33, Ephesians 5:11, 2 Corinthians 6:17

Laziness

Father, I come to you today for deliverance from laziness. I ask you to forgive me for giving in to the weakness of my flesh, which desires to be slothful, inactive, and lazy. My flesh is only concerned about its own comfort and does not desire to work or be productive. I realize that you created me to work and to be productive and fulfill your will on Earth. I cannot do that if I am yielding to the flesh and neglecting my responsibilities.

God, I desire to carry out your will and be busy with my Father's business just like Jesus. Right now, in the name of Jesus, I bind the spirit of laziness and command you to leave me now, as well as any other spirit such as depression, oppression, and fear that is operating in my life to keep me from being productive and fulfilling God's will. I disassociate myself from every person who would encourage me to be lazy. I remove from my possession every form of media that encourages or excuses a lifestyle of laziness. I declare today that I am no longer a lazy person. I am productive and active, and I take care of my responsibilities in a timely manner and complete all my tasks with excellence. I know God's will and what He has assigned to me, and I live every day of my life with great joy and excitement. I was created in Christ Jesus to do good works. I can do all things through Christ, who strengthens me. Father, I thank you today that I am free.

In Jesus' name, amen!

Scripture references

1 John 1:9, Proverbs 10:4, Matthew 25:26, Hebrews 6:12, Luke 2:49, Ephesians 2:10, Philippians 4:13, 1 Corinthians 15:33, Ephesians 5:11, 2 Corinthians 6:17

Low Self-Esteem

Father, I come to you today for deliverance from low self-esteem. Forgive me for believing the lies that have been spoken to me about myself. I have believed the lie that I am incapable, inadequate, and insufficient. That I am unimportant and unable to make a significant difference. The lies that I am not beautiful/handsome or attractive, and that I don't measure up to others.

Father, today I realize that these are all lies. Your word says that before you formed me in my mother's womb you already knew me. That you created me on purpose and with purpose. You have given me the ability to do everything you have planned for me, because Christ gives me strength. I will not compare my physical appearance to others, because I have been uniquely crafted by the hands of God.

Father, help me to discover how much you love me. Help me to know how precious I am to you, and how important I am in your master plan. Lead me on a journey discovering the gifts and callings you have given me. Allow me opportunities every day to do good to others and make a difference in their lives no matter how small it may seem. You created me in

Prayers that Bring Deliverance for Teens

Christ to do good works. Just as Christ went about in the power of the Spirit doing good works, I will do the same.

Today I make a conscious decision to change to way I view myself. No longer will I talk down on myself by making jokes or belittling myself. I realize these actions are an insult to you, my creator. I confess today that I am capable, sufficient, beautiful/handsome, intelligent, and every day I am making a positive difference in the lives of those around me. I disassociate myself from music, movies, magazines, books, TV shows, and all other media or objects that encourage low self-esteem. I will no longer subject myself to people who speak negative and hurtful lies over me that attempt to draw me back to low self-esteem. Right now, in the name of Jesus, I command the spirit of low self-esteem and every other associated spirit to leave me and never return. He whom the Son sets free is free indeed, and today I declare that I am free!

In Jesus' name, amen!

Scripture references
1 John 1:9, John 8:44, Jeremiah 1:5, 2 Timothy 3:16-17, Philippians 4:13, Ephesians 2:10, Acts 10:38, John 8:36, 1 Corinthians 15:33, Ephesians 5:11, 2 Corinthians 6:17

Lust

In the name of Jesus, I bind the spirit of lust and sexual perversion in my life. Father, first of all forgive me for allowing impure images and ideas to come into my mind through music, movies, television, conversation, pornography, or any other form of media. Forgive me for acting out on these thoughts through fornication, masturbation, molestation, homosexuality, bestiality, and any other form of perversion. I ask you to cleanse me today. Wash my mind with your word. Wash my heart with your blood and restore me to my rightful place in you.

Today I renounce lust and every form of sexual perversion. I acknowledge that my actions were sinful and detestable, and my heart is broken over my sin. You have given me a sexual desire, which is to be expressed in purity in marriage between a man and woman and not outside of those boundaries of safety and purity. I determine today to renew my mind by replacing every thought of lust and perversion by meditating on the pure word of God. I take authority over my life and will no longer allow impure thoughts to roam unchecked in my mind.

Today I remove from my possession every picture, movie, music, pornographic website, magazine, or association that would feed my carnal sexual desire and tempt me to sin.

Father, today I ask you to heal me in every broken place that has caused me to seek out sexual gratification in an unholy way. I also ask you to heal me from everything that sexual sin has broken in my life. Heal the people that I hurt, and heal relationships that have been broken. Heal my soul and break the power of every soul tie that has been established through sin.

Today I declare that I am forgiven, and I refuse to walk in guilt and shame. I am healed and filled with the love, joy, and peace of God. I am free and no longer a slave to lust and sexual perversion. I am free from the power of sin, and most of all I am free to live a life of purity and righteousness. I am free to live in pure fellowship with the men and women in my life and view them not as sexual objects, but with eyes of love and compassion as my Father in Heaven sees them.

In Jesus' name, amen!

Scripture references
1 John 1:9, Romans 13:13, Romans 12:2, Hebrews 13:4, 1 Corinthians 10:5, 1 Corinthians 6:13, Romans 8:1, 1 Timothy 5:2, 1 Corinthians 15:33, Ephesians 5:11, 2 Corinthians 6:17

Mental Illness

Father, in the name of Jesus, I come to you today for deliverance from the mental illness of _____ (name illness: schizophrenia, bipolar, multiple personality, confusion, indecisiveness, forgetfulness). Father I plead the blood of Jesus over my mind today and declare that when Jesus died on the cross He paid the price for my healing. He took the punishment I deserved so that I can receive salvation, healing, and deliverance. Sickness and disease are part of the curse that was brought about by Adam and Eve's sin in the Garden of Eden. When Jesus died, He removed the curse from me and made me a recipient of a new covenant, which includes health and healing. Since Jesus said that healing is the children's bread, I realize that I am entitled to healing.

Therefore, I declare today that I am healed of every type of mental illness or disorder _____ (name disorder). I declare that my mind is restored to a state of wholeness and I am no longer troubled by _____. I command every foul spirit that operates to cause confusion, indecision, and forgetfulness to lose my mind and let me go. I declare that

Prayers that Bring Deliverance for Teens

I have a sound mind. My thoughts are clear and precise, and I am able to make wise, confident decisions in a timely manner. I am able to process my thoughts and store them appropriately. I have control over my life. Your Holy Spirit is constantly bringing all things to my remembrance. I speak peace to my mind. No more stress, anxiety, or worry. I keep my mind on Christ, and He keeps me in perfect peace.

I command all spirits of bi-polar, schizophrenia, multiple personalities, etc., to come out of me now in the name of Jesus. You have been sent to destroy my life and keep me from fulfilling God's plan, but today your power over me ends. I repent of any sin of my own or generations before me that have made me vulnerable to these spirits. I ask for healing from traumatic events or life crises that opened the door for these spirits to come in. I forgive any and every individual or organization that hurt me. I declare that every door of my soul is closed to these spirits, and they will not have access to my seed and their generation.

Father, I seek you for total and complete healing of my soul. I will be diligent to renew my mind by studying and obeying your word. I will be faithful to daily times of prayer and worship and consistent church attendance. I thank you Father for setting me free. I declare that I am set free from this day forward and I will remember to give you all the praise.

In Jesus' name, amen!

Scripture references
1 Peter 2:24, Galatians 3:13, Matthew 15:26, John 14:26, 2 Timothy 1:7, Isaiah 26:3

Mother Wound

Father, today in the name of Jesus I come to you for healing and deliverance for the wounds I received from my natural mother. Father, I confess to you that my heart and soul have been wounded by my mother. I know that you are the God of all comfort and the mender of broken hearts; therefore, I open mine up to you and ask you to heal me, mend me, and make me whole. Heal me of all abuse and injustice my mother has either inflicted upon me or allowed others to inflict upon me. Wash away abusive words spoken in anger or rage. Replace them with your words of peace and loving kindness. Wash away words she spoke to me out of disappointment or disapproval. Replace them with words of approval and acceptance. Wash away the imprint left on my identity with hurtful or humiliating nicknames and replace them with your words of affirmation and identity. Heal me of the physical abuse she inflicted upon me. Heal my mind and remove the fear and timidity he instilled in me through her domineering or violent actions.

Fill the empty place she left in my heart by not being involved in my life. Bring peace to my mind that has been trying to understand why he left me or just was not interested in me.

Father, today I commit all these hurtful memories and experiences to you. I realize that I cannot compare you with my natural mother, who hurt and disappointed me. You are perfect and full of love and compassion. Therefore, I trust you with my heart and life. You said that when mother and father forsake me you would take me in. You said you are a father to the orphan; therefore, I trust you to fill the void that my mother left empty. Expose any unhealthy relationships that I am trying to use to fill the void my mother left through a lack of affection, approval, or presence in my life. Help me to seek you for complete healing and fulfillment.

Father, today I make the decision to forgive my mother. She is wrong for what she did, but I no longer hold her faults against her. Help me to see her for what she is: a soul that needs Jesus, who has experienced her own share of hurt and disappointment. Give me a heart of mercy and compassion for her. You instructed us to forgive others just as God through Christ has forgiven us; therefore, I forgive my mother because you have forgiven me. Lord, help me to sort through all the negative emotions associated with my mother. I realize that complete healing is a process and will take time, but I will trust you every step of the way. I lay aside all hatred, anger, resentment, bitterness, and any other negative emotion I have held toward her. I do not look to her for an apology or repayment for the wrongs she has committed against me. Lord, I look to you to restore to me what was taken or neglected.

Father, I ask you to bring about restoration with my mother. Help me to be obedient when you give me instructions. Give me words to say and actions to take for this God-ordained relationship to be restored. If my mother is deceased, help me find closure even though he is no longer with me.

Today I declare that I am healed, healthy, and whole. I am loved immensely by my Father in Heaven.

In Jesus' name, amen!

Scripture references
2 Corinthians 1:3-4, 2 Timothy 1:7, Romans 8:15, Psalm 27:10, Ephesians 4:32, Ecclesiastes 3:1-2

Offense

~❦~

Father, in the name of Jesus, I pray for deliverance from offense. First of all, I ask you to heal me of the hurt I have experienced due to this offense. I release all individuals who were involved in this situation (name each one), and I no longer hold them in my debt. I realize that they owe me nothing, and I am not looking to them to repay me for the wrongs they have committed. I realize that you have not withheld forgiveness from me; therefore, I must freely forgive others. I will no longer rehearse in my mind events, hurtful words, or situations that would nurse the offense, nor will I converse about it any longer. Not only do I forgive _____, but in the name of Jesus I bless them to prosper, to increase, to walk in love, joy, peace, and health. I pray that you would heal _____ of any hurt and offense they have encountered, and let the experience of your love and grace make them whole and complete.

I command the spirit of offense to leave me right now in the name of Jesus. I declare today that I am free from offense and any of its effects including bitterness, anger, self-pity, and resentment. I am free to love, free to give, and free to receive.

In Jesus' name, amen.

Scripture references
Proverbs 17:9, Romans 12:14, Ephesians 4:32

Pornography

Right now in the name of Jesus, I break the power of pornography over and in my life. I have been a slave of this demon for too long. Jesus came to destroy the works of the devil and set prisoners free, so today I plead the blood of Jesus over myself and command the spirit of pornography to leave me now. I renounce you. I am no longer in agreement with you. You are not a friend; you are an enemy that is slowly killing my soul. You have deceived and enticed me with pleasure and satisfaction, but after the thrill, you leave me drowning in an ocean of guilt, shame, regret, and darkness. Today I am breaking out of this prison. My soul is free! I declare that the glory light of Jesus Christ is shining in my soul and bringing light to every dark place. Every thought, every image, every scene of perversion and depravity I bring to the altar of my heart and lay them at the cross. Jesus became sin on the cross so that I could become the righteousness of God.

Father, today I am making a commitment to do whatever it takes to stay free. I will be held accountable by a mentor or spiritual leader whom I respect and who has a genuine concern for me. I remove from my possession every book, magazine, movie, picture, and poster that is pornographic or obscene in any way. I remove every file from my computer or other electronic device that contains pornographic material. I will not surf the Internet alone, but in the presence of someone who will hold me accountable. I disassociate myself from every person, club, or group that promotes, endorses, or excuses pornography. I declare that I am free from the bondage of pornography. Father, give me strength for the journey. Help me to walk everyday trusting in your grace. Let me be so intimate with you that the very thought of pornography is detestable and grieves my spirit. If I stumble or fall, help me not to allow condemnation to overtake me but instead to quickly confess my sins and continue pressing forward. Thank you, Lord, for setting me free!

In Jesus' name, amen!

Scripture references
1 John 1:9, 1 John 3:8, James 1:15, John 1:5, 2 Corinthians 5:21, Romans 5:17, 1 Corinthians 15:33, Ephesians 5:11, 2 Corinthians 6:17

Poverty

Father, in the name of Jesus, I come to you for deliverance from poverty. I realize that poverty is a curse and not a blessing. When you placed Adam and Eve in the Garden of Eden, you told them to be fruitful and multiply. You placed everything they needed in the garden and they lacked nothing. Therefore, I know it is not your will for me to lack and be in want. Jesus came so that I can have life and that more abundantly, and it is only Satan that desires to kill, steal, and destroy and bring loss, lack, and decrease in my life. In the book of Genesis, you blessed Abraham abundantly and caused him to be very wealthy in silver, gold, and livestock. Therefore, since I am Abraham's seed I declare that the blessing of the Lord has made me rich as well.

Today I renounce poverty. My family and generations before me may have lived in and accepted poverty as a lifestyle, but today I declare that curse is broken in my life and the lives of my children. Spirit of poverty, I command you to leave me now in the name of Jesus. I am no longer in agreement with you and the lies you used to convince me that

I have no hope of prospering. Today I declare that I am prospering financially.

Father, I ask you to help me renew my mind concerning finances. Expose and remove every inappropriate thought I have concerning money. Teach me your principals for financial success. Teach me to be diligent in my work, for the hand of the diligent will prosper. Teach me to be a tither and a giver and to honor you with everything I have. Teach me to think prosperous thoughts. Help me to cast out every thought that promotes poverty, stinginess, and greed. Remove the fear of not having enough and running out that causes me to hold tightly to what I have. Help me to understand that you are the God of more than enough. I will trust you to supply over and above all my needs so that I am in a position to help others. Teach me to live debt free, owing nothing to any man but to love him. Your word says that I am the lender and not the borrower, for the borrower is always a slave to the lender.

Help me to remove myself from people who are determined to be poor, think poor, act poor, and talk poor, and those who are always blaming others for their lack of success. I know that if God is for me, who can be against me? Let me surround myself with people who are determined to live according to the word of God in fullness and abundance.

Today I declare that I am free from poverty. I am not discouraged by my circumstances, nor am I dictated by them. I am blessed, because God says I am blessed. I am increasing day by day, because the blessing of the Lord makes me rich and adds no sorrow. Lord, as you increase me I will be sure to continually give all praise and honor and glory to you. Use me as a testimony and a financial deliverer to set others free from poverty.

In Jesus' name, amen!

Scripture references
1 John 1:9, Deuteronomy 28, Genesis 9:7, Psalm 23, John 10:10, Genesis 13:2, Galatians 3:7, Romans 12:2, Proverbs 12:24, Malachi 3:10, Romans 3:18, Deuteronomy 28:12, Romans 8:31, 1 Corinthians 15:33, Ephesians 5:11,
2 Corinthians 6:17

Pride

Father, I come to you today for deliverance from the spirit of pride. I confess that a proud heart is a sinful heart, and I ask you to forgive me for this sin of pride. I realize that pride will only lead me to destruction and cause me to fall in shame and disgrace. I know that you resist those who are proud and self-sufficient, but you give grace to the humble.

Father, today I ask you to give me a heart of humility. I have used pride as a protective shield to guard my heart, which is actually fearful and insecure. But today I realize that I do not have to protect myself. You are my shield and defense. You will keep and protect me. You will not let evil overcome me. You will not allow my foot to stumble. I do not have to fight or defend myself.

Today I put my trust in you and not in my own strength and ability. I am free to be still and see your power working for me. Not only am I free to trust in you, but I am also free to receive help from other people. I am also free to receive instruction, correction, and discipline from others. I admit that I don't know as much as I think I do. I can't do everything that I claim, and I am not always right. I am able to humble myself and admit my wrongs and ask for forgiveness from others.

Today I disassociate myself from pride. I am not in agreement with proud thoughts. I will daily renew my mind with the truth of God's word so that I will be transformed into a person who walks humbly before God and others. Right now, in the name of Jesus, I command the spirit of pride to leave me along with every other spirit that is associated such as _____, _____, _____(name them here).

I declare today that I am free from the spirit and attitude of pride. I am washed in the blood of Jesus, and my mind is renewed with His word. I thank you, Father, that you have set me free, and I am free indeed!

In Jesus' name, amen!

Scripture references
1 John 1:9, Proverbs 16:18, Psalm 7:10, Psalm 121:3, Romans 12:2, 1 Corinthians 15:33, Ephesians 5:11, 2 Corinthians 6:17

Rebellion

Right now, in the name of Jesus, I bind the spirit of rebellion from operating in my life. Father, I ask you to forgive me for yielding myself to the spirit of rebellion and causing discord, confusion, hurt, and offense in the lives and organizations of those I am associated with. I recognize that this is the spirit of Satan, and I will aggressively stand against its operation in my life.

I pray, Father, that you will heal me at the root, which is expressed through rebellion. Remove all fear from my heart that causes me to resist authority for fear that they will take advantage of me. My trust is in you, and I will not be put to shame. Remove all selfishness from my heart that only allows me to think of my own needs and wants. Help me to think of the greater good and work together with others under their leadership. Heal me of all rejection I have experienced, which causes me to push others away and reject relationships before they ever begin. Wash my heart of every attitude that is negative and rebellious. Give me a heart that is agreeable and not contrary.

Today I renounce the spirit of rebellion and everything associated with it. I sever every relationship that would promote or nurture a spirit of rebellion. I remove from my possession all books, magazine, music, movies, TV shows, and anything else that promotes rebellion. Today I am free to live in submission and respect toward those who are in authority over me. My thoughts and actions foster an atmosphere of peace, unity, love, and agreement, and everywhere I go I am a blessing to all that I come in contact with.

In Jesus' name amen!

Scripture references
1 John 1:9, 1 Samuel 15:23, 1 Corinthians 15:33, Ephesians 5:11, 2 Corinthians 6:17

Religion

Father, today in the name of Jesus, I come to you for deliverance from the spirit of religion. Father, forgive me for having an appearance of Godliness, but not allowing the true power of God to transform my heart. I have a desire to be righteous, but I have not trusted in you to make me righteous. I have developed a form of self-righteousness and depended on my own religious works and efforts to make me right in your eyes. Father, today I realize that I am saved by grace through faith in Jesus Christ, not of my own good works; therefore, I have no right to be proud for my righteousness comes from you alone.

Father, forgive me for becoming proud and thinking that my way is the only right way. Help me to live my own life based on the revelation of the word you have given me and allow others to live and grow according to the revelation you have given them. Forgive me for judging and criticizing those who do not conduct themselves according to my personal standards. Forgive me for exalting my church or denomination and allowing it to become an idol and a source of pride. Forgive me for exalting my own opinion, tradition, and church doctrine above your word.

Today I bring all these things and lay them at your feet. Anything that is not based on your word I acknowledge as my own personal opinion and conviction, and I will not condemn others for not conforming to my ways.

Father, I realize that is was the spirit of religion that caused the religious leaders to kill Jesus, because they were not able to understand what God was doing through Jesus. Help me not to stand or speak against the move of your Spirit, even though I may not understand it.

Father, remove a heart of judgment, pride, and criticism, and give me a heart of love and mercy. Let me have the mind of Christ. A willingness to humble myself and love and serve others. I realize I cannot win the lost by hating and judging them, but by allowing God's loving kindness to be expressed through me and by speaking the truth of Jesus Christ in love. Help me to live my life as an example to other believers and restore with meekness those who are in scriptural error, realizing that I also have the ability to stumble and fall.

Father, right now in the name of Jesus, I bind and cast out the spirit of religion and every other spirit associated with it: pride, hatred, criticism, insecurity, _____, _____(name others here).

Today I renounce the spirit of religion. You will no longer use me to bring division, criticism, and hatred to the people that God loves. Today I declare that I am free. Since I have repented of my sin, times of refreshing are coming to me, and my relationship with my savior is being renewed and restored.

In Jesus' name, amen!

Scripture references
1 John 1:9, 1 Timothy 3:5, Ephesians 2:8, Romans 14:13, Colossians 2:8, Philippians 2:5, Ephesians 6:20, Jeremiah 31:3, Ephesians 4:15, 1 Timothy 4:12, Galatians 6:1, 1 Corinthians 15:33, Ephesians 5:11, 2 Corinthians 6:17

Self-Mutilation

Father, in the name of Jesus I come to you today for deliverance from self-mutilation. First of all, I ask you to forgive me for abusing my body, which is your temple. I realize it is not your will for me to treat myself in this way. Father, I ask you now to heal my heart. Reach deep inside of me and heal all the pain that I am feeling inside (list hurts and pains). Heal me of all hurt, rejection, grief, abandonment, anger, sorrow, and any other negative emotion.

Today I make the decision to forgive myself for every bad decision that I've made. Even when I suffered at the hands of others, I do not hold myself responsible for what they did to me. They had no right to hurt me. I release myself, and I declare that I am no longer angry or disappointed with myself. I know that you love and forgive me freely; therefore, I am able to love and forgive myself. I love myself. I am made in God's own image. He formed me in my mother's womb and placed me on this earth, because He has a specific and special plan for me.

Today I renounce self-mutilation. I command every foul spirit that is associated with self-mutilation to come out of me now. Spirit of self-hatred, vio-

Self-mutilation

lence, anger, guilt, grief, condemnation, depression, suicide, and any other evil spirit that influenced me to abuse myself to come out now in Jesus' name. I will no longer associate myself with people who would tempt me to sin in this way. I remove from my possession all dark music, clothing, art, books, poetry, and any other article or form of media that would produce an atmosphere of oppression and darkness. I also remove from my possession all objects I have used to harm myself. I declare that I am free from every hurtful memory. Even though I can still recall the events, they no longer have power over my actions and emotions, causing me to mutilate my own body.

Today I declare that I am set free by the blood of Jesus. My heart is healed, my mind is renewed, and every burden is lifted!

In Jesus' name, amen!

Scripture references
1 John 1:9, 1 Corinthians 6:19, Ephesians 4:32, Jeremiah 1:5, Genesis 1:27, 1 Corinthians 15:33, Ephesians 5:11, 2 Corinthians 6:17

Soul Ties

Father, today in the name of Jesus I break the power of unhealthy soul ties in my life. I sever all unhealthy connections with _____ (name of person or organization) that are hindering me in my thoughts and my emotions. You said not to be unequally joined with people who are not believers. Even though my relationship with _____ may have been enjoyable and even beneficial for me at one time, this relationship has become a hindrance now that I am living as a disciple in obedience to your word. I love _____ and will continually pray for them, but today I renounce all deep and intimate connections with _____. I will no longer nurture thoughts, emotions, or activities that would strengthen this relationship. I also loosen myself from relationships that have ended willingly or unwillingly, or relationships that I am having difficulty letting go of. Your word says that there is a time and a season for everything under the sun, so I thank you for the season that you allowed me to enjoy a relationship with _____, but today I acknowledge that season is over whether I want it to be or not, and I make the conscious decision to

Soul Ties

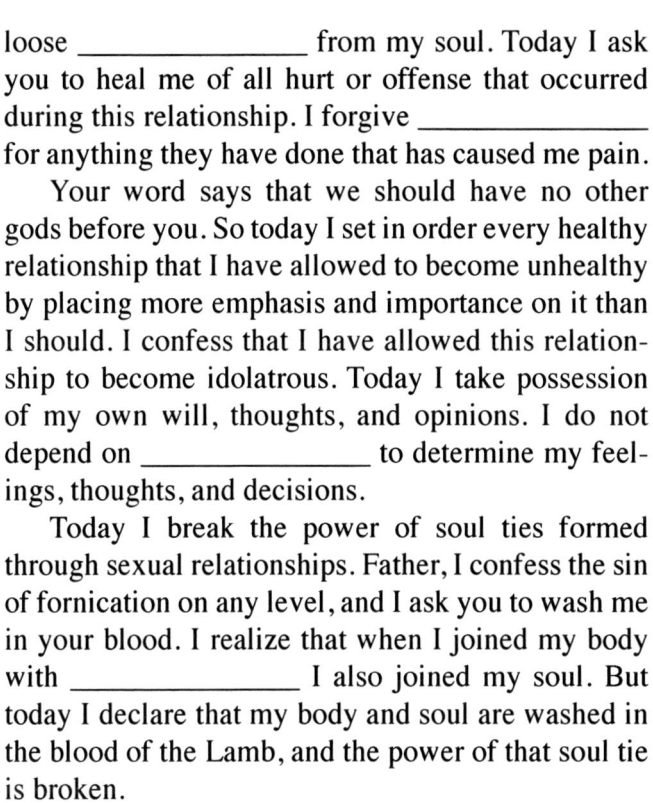

loose _____ from my soul. Today I ask you to heal me of all hurt or offense that occurred during this relationship. I forgive _____ for anything they have done that has caused me pain.

Your word says that we should have no other gods before you. So today I set in order every healthy relationship that I have allowed to become unhealthy by placing more emphasis and importance on it than I should. I confess that I have allowed this relationship to become idolatrous. Today I take possession of my own will, thoughts, and opinions. I do not depend on _____ to determine my feelings, thoughts, and decisions.

Today I break the power of soul ties formed through sexual relationships. Father, I confess the sin of fornication on any level, and I ask you to wash me in your blood. I realize that when I joined my body with _____ I also joined my soul. But today I declare that my body and soul are washed in the blood of the Lamb, and the power of that soul tie is broken.

Today I stand and declare that I am free from every unhealthy soul tie. All grief, sorrow, and regret are removed. I reclaim every part of my soul that was still attached to individuals who are no longer in my life. I declare that I am whole and ready to enter into new, healthy relationships that God has ordained for me. I declare that all of my relationships are healthy and in proper balance, and only God can sit on the throne of my heart. I am ready for my next level, and I embrace this new season in my life.

In Jesus' name, amen!

Scripture references
1 John 1:9, 2 Corinthians 6:14, Ecclesiastes 3:1, Exodus 20:3, 1 Corinthians 6:15-20, 1 Corinthians 15:33, Ephesians 5:11, 2 Corinthians 6:17

Suicide
(pray in conjunction with Depression)

Father, in the name of Jesus I rebuke the spirit of suicide from my life. I take authority over the darkness that has infiltrated my life, and by faith I release the light of Jesus Christ to shine in my life and overtake the darkness. I command the spirit of suicide to be silenced. Leave my room, my home, and any other place you are lingering. I am no longer under your influence. I will not entertain thoughts of violating God's law by taking my own life. Death is not the answer. God's thoughts for me are of peace and not evil to give me a future and hope. I close every door that has allowed the demonic to be activated in my life. I remove all books, magazines, movies, TV shows, and objects that promote suicide or depression. I remove from my possession the items I was considering using to commit suicide. I am free from suicidal thoughts and desires. I declare that I will live and not die and declare the works of the Lord.

In Jesus' name, amen!

Scripture references
1 John 1:9, John 1:5, 1 Corinthians 15:33, Ephesians 5:11, 2 Corinthians 6:17

Witchcraft/Occult

Father, in the name of Jesus I come to you for deliverance from witchcraft and the occult. First of all, I ask you Father to forgive me for opening the door to Satan through demonic (something that promotes evil or spirituality without Jesus) movies, TV shows, games, music, books, literature, séances, fortune telling, art, or any other avenue. Father, I ask you to forgive my family members _____ (names) for opening a spiritual door that has now affected my life.

Father, I plead the blood of your Son Jesus over me, and I declare that I am cloaked in your grace. Jesus said all power is in His hand, and He has given me His power and authority to cast out demons. Jesus came to destroy the works of the devil and His work is finished. Therefore, I declare today that Satan's work is destroyed in my life. Today, in the name of Jesus, I renounce all associations with Satan and his kingdom. I don't want anything to do with witchcraft or darkness of any kind. I command the spirit of witchcraft and every foul spirit that is associated with it to come out of me now in the name of Jesus. I do not want you. I am not in agreement with and I am no longer consenting to your presence in my life. Therefore, I command you to leave and never return to me again.

I have been translated into God's kingdom, which is a kingdom of light. I declare that the light of God's glory is infiltrating my body, soul, and spirit and filling every dark place so that the darkness is not able to remain. Today my countenance and disposition has restored to reflect the light of Jesus, which dwells abundantly in me.

Today I remove from my possession all movies, TV shows, clothing, makeup, music, books, art, literature, and artifacts of any kind that would attract or project unclean spirits or temp me to sin. I sever all relationships with people _____(names) or groups and affiliations _____(name) that are involved in these dark practices. I declare today that I am free from the powers and influence of darkness by the power of God through Christ Jesus. The power of God is greater than any other, and He has given Jesus a name that is above every name. Greater is He that is in me than he that is in the world; therefore, I do not fear retaliation nor will I be intimidated. Jesus is lord of my life, and I am submitted and obedient to Him. His love, power, and grace are at work in my life. Because of His great and unconditional love for me, I will serve Him all of my days.

Father, I praise you today. You delivered me. I am so thankful for the freedom and liberty I now have in you. I will fill myself with music that praises and glorifies God, with books that bring revelation of God, with movies and television shows that are clean and uplifting, with clothes that express the joy and freedom God has given, and with friends that will encourage me to draw closer to God and live a life of holiness and purity.

In Jesus' name, amen!

Scripture references
I John 1:9, Deuteronomy 18:10, Matthew 28:18, Matthew 10:1, 1 John 3:8, Colossians 1:13, John 8:12, Philippians 2:9, 1 Corinthians 15:33, Ephesians 5:11, 2 Corinthians 6:17

Conclusion

There is no greater power on earth than the power of prayer! You now have the tools you need to consistently live a victorious life. Although you may have already read through these prayers, don't put the book down too soon. Continue to use these prayers on a daily basis to reinforce the victory you have gained. Read the scriptures references to help build your faith and further equip you for your journey. If you happen to find yourself in bondage again remember that the same God that set you free before can do it again!

This is my prayer for you: Father, I pray for each one that had the courage to confront their sins, struggles and addictions. I pray that you continue to bless them with a mind to walk in victory. Continue to show them that your grace is sufficient for them. Most of all let each one be rooted and grounded, firmly established in your love.

In Jesus' mighty name, amen!

CPSIA information can be obtained
at www.ICGtesting.com
Printed in the USA
FFOW03n2056160218
45147960-45624FF

9 781624 196690